BOY SCOUTS OF AMERICA
MERIT BADGE SERIES

PUBLIC SPEAKING

 BOY SCOUTS OF AMERICA®

Requirements

1. Give a three- to five-minute introduction of yourself to an audience such as your troop, class at school, or some other group.

2. Prepare a three- to five-minute talk on a topic of your choice that incorporates body language and visual aids.

3. Give an impromptu talk of at least two minutes either as part of a group discussion or before your counselor. Use a subject selected by your counselor that is interesting to you but that is not known to you in advance and for which you do not have time to prepare.

4. Select a topic of interest to your audience. Collect and organize information about the topic and prepare an outline. Write an eight- to 10-minute speech, practice it, then deliver it in a conversational way.

5. Show you know parliamentary procedure by leading a discussion or meeting according to accepted rules of order, or by answering questions on the rules of order.

35936
ISBN 978-0-8395-3373-3
©2002 Boy Scouts of America
2011 Printing

BANG/Brainerd, M
8-2011/06258

Contents

You Are a Public Speaker!

You might not think of yourself as a public speaker, but every time you speak to a group of your friends, classmates, or at a Scout meeting, you are presenting yourself and your views in public. Even if you haven't stood at a podium on the stage and find the whole idea scary, sooner or later, someone is going to ask you to get up and say a few words. If you are prepared, it won't be scary. It can even be fun.

One day you might be asked to give a toast at your best friend's wedding or speak in front of your local community about something you believe in strongly. You might have to lead a formal business meeting or speak at the worst of times, such as someone's funeral. A lot happens during the course of every person's life, and your ability to communicate your feelings and ideas is the best way to connect to the larger world.

After you have earned the Public Speaking merit badge, you can go further into the field by earning the Communications merit badge. But for now: "Thank you for being here, Scouts and Venturers. Our topic today is public speaking. . . . "

Learning to carry yourself well, speak effectively in public, listen carefully, and understand the needs of the audience are important skills that can help you throughout your life.

Four Main Types of Speeches

The four main types of speeches are: informative, entertaining, convincing, and persuasive.

Inform Them

An *informative* speech presents the facts. It informs and instructs the audience on a topic it might not know much about without attempting to change the audience's opinions of the topic.

Let's say you are giving an informative speech to your troop on no-trace camping techniques. Telling a story about the history of your topic is a good way to begin. You could explain that no-trace camping was practiced by American Indian tribes who have called this country home for thousands of years. Then explain the importance of no-trace camping, particularly when you are trekking in pristine wilderness areas. In the body of the speech, present detailed information about how to camp and cook out for an extended period without leaving even a footprint behind.

Visual aids help the audience understand what you mean. For example, hold up pictures of various brands of freeze-dried food packets and energy bars that you have tried and can recommend. Or show examples of lightweight cooking and camping gear Scouts can use to make the most of a backcountry experience.

Finally, end your speech with a quote by a famous naturalist or wildlife photographer that drives home your point: Leave nothing behind except memories.

Entertain Them

To *entertain* doesn't necessarily mean to be funny, but most entertaining speeches are. Studies show that audiences like speakers who use humor, and information that is presented in a funny way, such as a joke or personal anecdote, tends to be remembered longer. Humor also helps build rapport with the audience. But, to use it successfully, keep your joke or funny story short and relevant to your speech. In other words, use humor to make a point.

Funny quotes are a great way to get attention. A quote by an important person who boldly made a prediction that turned out to be, well, dead wrong, makes a point about how things change. Take for instance, Charles H. Duell, director of the U.S. Patent Office in 1899, who is credited with saying more than 100 years ago, "Everything that can be invented has been invented." Or Lord Kelvin, president of The Royal Society, who predicted in 1895 that "heavier-than-air flying machines are impossible." Quotes like these drive home the difference between then and now. You could even take the joke a step further by saying, "Of course, I was just a boy at that time. . . ."

Some people like to use Murphy's Law: "Anything that can go wrong, will go wrong." You can use this funny observation to your advantage in telling a joke.

Poking a little fun at yourself is another way to score points with audiences. But don't go overboard or put yourself down. For example, put people at ease by teasing them about how long you plan to talk: "When I asked Scoutmaster Martin what I should talk about today, he said, with a fierce gaze, 'Talk about five minutes.'"

Convince Them

A speech to *convince* attempts to influence the audience's attitude toward the material presented. The speech seeks to make the audience believe or accept your point of view, or stimulate or inspire your audience. For instance, let's say you live in an urban neighborhood. Your city council wants to turn your only neighborhood basketball court into a much-needed parking lot. You decide to give a speech to your class about how much the basketball court means to you and your friends.

Every element you put into this speech should aim to convince youths your age, regardless of whether they play basketball, that losing this play space would be harmful to your whole community. Your goal is to call attention to this issue and inspire the audience to care about the basketball court as much as you do.

Relate how many youths play hoops there daily and present statistics from the local police department that show how much petty crime among local youth has declined since the basketball court was built. Cite the lack of playground facilities in your area, or how many students who once played at the local court went on to play high school and/or college basketball. Tell about someone you know (without using a real name) who might have gotten involved with the wrong crowd if not for the respect and self-confidence learned on the basketball court.

If you are passionate about an issue, regardless of what it is, the key to convincing others is to be honest and find intelligent ways to make your point through research, personal stories, humor, quotations, statistics, and facts.

Persuade Them to Action

A speech that *persuades to action* seeks an active response. The goal is to motivate listeners to do more than merely believe in the topic being presented—they should act on it! This could mean voting a certain way, signing a petition, or changing a behavior.

Think about the immediacy and sheer power of the following seven words: "Give me liberty or give me death!" Those "fighting words" were shouted defiantly by Colonial American statesman Patrick Henry in 1775. The zeal with which his message spread throughout the country inspired colonists to unite against an oppressive British monarchy. There was a price to pay in blood, yet the 13 colonies became something new: the free and democratic United States of America.

Your persuasive speech need not be this dramatic or cover this big a subject. For example, write a speech to persuade people to clean up a local creek, or to rally your troop to help build a ramp for a neighbor who is disabled. You could ask people to raise funds for a local skateboard park or encourage youths to volunteer in your community.

But for the moment, consider Patrick Henry an expert on persuading people to action. Here is the last paragraph of his rallying speech that called a nation to arms:

"Gentlemen may cry, Peace, Peace—but there is no peace. The war is actually begun! The next gale that sweeps from the north will bring to our ears the clash of resounding arms! Our brethren are already in the field! Why stand we here idle? What is it that gentlemen wish? What would they have? Is life so dear, or peace so sweet, as to be purchased at the price of chains and slavery? Forbid it, Almighty God! I know not what course others may take; but as for me, give me liberty or give me death!"

Getting Started

Now think about the purpose of the speech you will give. The first step is to gather ideas and jot them down. Don't just sit down and try to write a speech cold turkey. Once you get your ideas down, you will be able to flush out the details of your speech—no problem! Here are eight different ways to organize your ideas.

Chronological Order

A talk organized into past, present, and future categories is easy to follow. If you are speaking about yourself or a series of events, try organizing your ideas chronologically.

Problem and Solution

Simply state a problem and offer a solution. When a speech is organized this way, what you say depends on how much the audience already knows about the issue. For example, if the audience is well-informed, focus most of your speech on the solution.

Analogy or Metaphor

When you compare your ideas to a similar object or idea, you create a picture that helps the audience understand how your ideas are related. For example, author Malcolm Kushner compares giving a speech to the flight of an airplane, complete with the takeoff, or introduction; the flight, or body of the speech; the passengers, or audience; the pilot, or speaker; and the landing, or conclusion.

Cause and Effect

This organizational pattern is useful for scientific discussions. Just state a problem or situation, what caused it to happen, and trace what the impact has been.

Divide a Word

Find a word that mirrors your ideas in such a way that you can use it as an acronym, or mnemonic device, to make your main points easy to remember. For example: "Take the word 'Life.' *L* stands for love of family, *I* stands for the question of infinite wisdom, *F* stands for forgiveness, a very important quality to possess, and *E* stands for the energy to do great things."

Mine a Phrase

Here is an example of how you can mine a phrase to introduce your ideas: "Filmmaker Woody Allen once said, 'I wouldn't want to be a member of any group that would have me as a member.' I felt that way, too, until I found Scouting, or rather . . . until Scouting found me. You see, my dad signed me up for Boy Scouts when I was 9, and since then, I've had such a great time and learned so much being a member of this troop. . . ."

Segment a Topic

Divide your topic into segments based on your own organizational pattern. Suppose you are giving a speech on how a Scout camp is laid out. You might divide the topic into (1) waterfront area, (2) campsite, (3) trading post, (4) archery area, and (5) Scoutcraft area.

Brain Strain

If you can't seem to get started, brainstorm ideas with friends, family members, your Scoutmaster, teachers, or local experts. No matter what your topic, there are probably people you can ask for advice on the subject. And don't forget librarians. The reference desk at your local library is always a great (and free!) place to ask about any subject.

How to Avoid Hypothermia

1. Stay warm and dry.

2. Stay well-hydrated.

3. Eat high-energy foods.

4. Take regular rest stops.

5. Watch fellow Backpackers
   for signs of hypothermia.

Keep your numerical list and tips short.

Numerical List

Some experts believe numerical lists are the most powerful way to organize information. Magazine editors also recognize the lure of lists. Just look at the following magazine headlines: "The Top 10 Day Trips You Can Take With Your Kids," "Five Ways to Lose Weight Now," "The Best Six Little Toys You'll Ever Give for Christmas."

If you organize your speech this way—"I have four good ideas to present to you today"—you will grab the audience's immediate attention. As long as you keep the list *short,* the audience will count the points as you make them.

Here are a few ways to organize ideas for the body of your speech. Remember, each idea you write down should be related to the next idea and to your topic. As you jot things down, you will find that ideas group naturally. Once your idea are divided into the various points you want to cover, you can build the speech from there.

Use Quotes, Anecdotes, and Statistics to Drive Home Main Points

No matter what the topic is, once you have the main points, you need to find a good angle or angles for fleshing out the information in an interesting way. Mining reference materials is a good way to find quotes, statistics, offbeat facts, and other tools to spice up your speech. Basic reference tools at the library include almanacs, dictionaries, and encyclopedias.

• Check out what other intelligent people have said about your topic in *Bartlett's Familiar Quotations.*

• For statistics, try *The New York Times Almanac.* For general information, browse the Readers' Guide to Periodical Literature or The New York Times Index.

• Need offbeat facts? How about the *Guinness World Records* book?

Now get in gear and build the body of your speech with the same integrity as you would build a model airplane. Go to the library or connect to the Internet. Interview experts or mine yourself for information, insights, and observations. Read books and articles, or visit a museum. In other words, leave no stone unturned.

Research the Web

Online, check out the following helpful websites (with your parent's permission, of course):

- Need to tackle a subject? Refdesk (http://www.refdesk.com) is a great place to research topics.

- Looking for a powerful search engine to find information on a topic? Both Search Thingy (http://www.searchthingy.com/search.asp) and Dogpile (http://www.dogpile.com) scour several top search engines and display the top listings. Another solid search engine is Google (http://www.google.com).

- Need a newspaper article? NewsLink (http://newslink.org/) maintains a large list of newspaper, magazine, and TV station websites organized by topic and geographic location.

- *Bartlett's Familiar Quotations* is online at http://www.bartleby.com/100.

- Need a myth or legend to make a point? Story Arts Online (http://www.storyarts.org) is a good place to search for stories from around the world.

- Do you want to see what famous Americans said in their speeches? Check out the Douglass Archives of American Public Address (http://douglassarchives.org). The U.S. Department of Defense keeps a vault of military speeches at http://www.defenselink.mil/speeches.

- A good source for speech transcripts and audiovisual resources can be found at the Speech and Transcript Center (http://www.freepint.com/gary/speech.htm).

When to Use an Outline

The longer the speech, the more you need an outline. Think of an outline as a map to guide you through each part of your speech. A speech naturally divides into three parts: the introduction, body, and conclusion. You can start outlining any one of these three sections; it isn't necessary to tackle them in chronological order. Generally it is best to work on the body first, then on the introduction and the conclusion. Here is the order of presentation so you can see how each part of the speech fits in.

INTRODUCTION

During your introduction, accomplish the following three things:

1. Recognize the person who introduced you.

2. Voice your appreciation for the chance to speak before the group.

3. Arouse interest in the subject by letting the audience know where you hope to take them.

The introduction should be long enough to do the job but no longer. If your audience is familiar with you and your subject, you hardly need any introduction at all.

BODY

This is the main part of the speech. Develop each idea on your list, illustrating the main points with a variety of information, including facts, opinions, reasons, quotes, examples, personal stories, analogies, or statistics—these are the building blocks of any good speech.

CONCLUSION

The conclusion rounds off your speech and gets you back to your seat. Keep it short and simple, and use it to sum up arguments and appeal for action from the audience. This is not the only way to conclude a speech, but it is the most frequently used way.

Sample Outline

Let's say you are giving a speech to boys who are not Scouts on the value of Scouting. Your purpose is to *convince* them to join your troop by telling them how fun and exciting Scouting is. Your topic will be, in one sentence, "Scouting is fun and helps boys become valuable citizens and leaders in their community." Begin working on your idea list, adding all of your thoughts on the values of Scouting. When you have them written down, eliminate the weakest arguments.

Next comes the outline, which might look like the following:

Introduction
Thank the person who introduced you.
State your appreciation for the chance to speak.
State your argument or topic briefly.

Body
I. Scouting provides citizenship training
   a. By teaching boys to live and work together
   b. By teaching skills useful in helping others, such as first aid
   c. By stressing our American heritage in its activities
   d. By teaching respect for patriotic symbols such as the flag

II. Scouting develops character
   a. By teaching Scouts to live by the Scout Oath and Law
   b. Through service projects and Good Turns
   c. By teaching skills that emphasize self-reliance and preparedness

III. Scouting develops physical and mental fitness
   a. Through outdoor activities
   b. By patrol competition
   c. By providing standards of physical fitness by which a Scout can measure himself

Notice that this speech was developed so that the most important point—"Scouting is fun!"—comes last. This way, the best ammunition is saved for last so that the audience is still thinking about it before the speaker calls them to action: Join up!

Remember, the outline is not the speech. It's just the skeleton on which you can hang all the supporting facts, personal stories, opinions, and examples.

IV. Scouting is fun!
   a. It offers camping and hiking.
   b. Scouts learn many outdoor skills.
   c. It offers swimming, canoeing, and boating.
   d. It gives boys a chance to do things with their friends.

Conclusion
Summarize the four main points.
Make an appeal for boys to join.

Get Rid of Stage Fright

Ulp. Stage fright. Everyone goes through it. It made The Beatles toss their cookies before concerts. It kept singer Barbra Streisand from performing in public for 10 years. What if you can't do it? What if you get in front of an audience and seize, can't say a word, or shake like a leaf in a strong wind?

Relax. The first step to overcoming stage fright is to realize everyone—from presidents to film stars to preachers—goes through it. And you can overcome it. The Advanced Public Speaking Institute in Landover Hills, Maryland, recommends the following techniques for overcoming your fears:

• Before you go on stage, take a few deep breaths and yawn to relax your throat. Close your eyes and picture the audience listening, laughing, and applauding.

- Concentrate on how good you are at public speaking.

- Pretend you are just chatting with a group of friends.

- Be prepared—memorize your opening lines so you can recite these on autopilot if you must.

- Practice, practice, practice! Practice enough so that no matter how nervous you are, you can spit out a few minutes of your program.

- If you feel shaky on stage, don't hold the notes in your hands: the audience can see them fluttering. Instead, hold on to the lectern. If your legs start to wobble, lean one knee against the lectern while you hold on to the top part of it with your hands.

Here are more tips to banish stage fright, from professional speaker Chris Widener.

- Focus on getting through the first five minutes of your speech. Rarely do you see anyone who is afraid through the entire speech. Usually the speaker settles in and becomes comfortable after the first few minutes.

- Remember that you are your own worst critic. Widener recalls seeing a group of his friends who played in a band perform at a hot club in New York City. Afterward, the band members moaned that they had played "terribly." Widener didn't think so and neither did the audience. Most people are not coming to hear you speak with the goal of picking you apart. So don't pick yourself apart either!

- Understand that most people in the audience would be scared to death to get up and give a speech, and they are glad it is you and not them. For the occasional speaker, it's OK to say, "Excuse my nerves, I'm not used to this." It's one way to get the audience on your side.

Organizing Your Speech

It's time to write your speech. If you have thought about the topic clearly, jotted down your ideas, and possibly prepared an outline, you are ready to write.

Introduction: The Most Important Part

When you first get up to speak, you will receive better attention from the audience than at any other time until you finish. The first and last sentences or paragraphs in a speech are the easiest for the audience to remember, so make your introductory comments memorable.

A **question** has an unfinished feeling that demands further attention. It creates an air of expectancy. For instance, you might begin a speech about Scouting by asking, "Could you go into the deep woods tonight with just a pocketknife, a couple of matches, and a blanket, and live fairly comfortably for a week or more?" You don't really expect an answer: This is what is known as a rhetorical question. Your point in asking the question is to heighten interest in Scouting by implying that if the listeners were Scouts, they would know this important set of survival skills.

Startling or far-fetched statements quickly seize the audience's interest, too. A dramatic opening has the same effect, as long as the story is relevant to the subject. Let's say you live in an area of the Midwest known as Tornado Alley for its deadly tornadoes.

Seven Keys

Here are some ways you can unlock an audience's interest from the get-go. Use one to introduce your subject.

1. A question

2. A startling statement

3. A personal experience

4. Something familiar

5. Humor

6. A historic survey

7. A myth, legend, quote, or short story

You have decided to give a speech to your class about the history of these killer storms in your area and important ways people can stay safe.

You could begin with a dramatic story about the last tornado that touched down in your county: "Calvin and Doris Denny had just curled up on the couch to watch TV the stormy night of September 4, 1999. Suddenly the house went dark, their living room window shattered into a thousand pieces of jagged shrapnel, and their truck, which moments before had been parked in the street, was hurled into their kitchen like a matchbox toy."

This startling story contrasts sharply with the audience's immediate situation. Sharp contrasts increase curiosity among listeners and makes them sit up and take notice.

Recounting a **personal experience** relevant to the subject can bring you and the audience closer together.

Start with a **familiar** quotation—"What goes up must come down!"—and the audience will finish it almost audibly for you, without your asking.

Humor is another good way to introduce a subject, as long as your joke is funny and relevant. Stay clear of ethnic slurs, off-color remarks, and anything offensive. Often, humor aimed gently at yourself is the best way for folks to identify with you.

A brief **historical survey** can be an effective opening when the speech is about new developments in a specific field. For example, if you were talking about the hazards of space flight, you might begin by pointing out that Orville and Wilbur Wright faced no hazards much worse than broken bones at Kitty Hawk in 1903. Today's astronauts face countless dangers.

Everyone loves a good **story** well-told. If you can find a story connected to your topic, it can be an excellent way to lead into the body of your speech.

Body: The Meat and Potatoes

Develop the main points in this section. Each idea, as it is presented, must be supported by facts, reasons, examples, or opinions gathered in your research.

Typically, each point should be supported by three examples. Use statistics, personal stories, analogies, quotes, or whatever best illustrates the point you want to make.

The main points should be presented in logical order. They also should be tied together. When moving from one

> A typical speech contains three to five main points. The audience will judge the importance a speaker places on a particular point by how much time is spent on that point. You should, too, in planning the time you will spend on each main point.

point to another, use a transitional phrase to pull your listener along to the next part of the speech. Make smooth transitions using phrases such as the following:

- "On another point . . . "

- "To summarize . . . "

- "Now let's take a look at . . . "

- "In addition . . . "

- "The next point is . . . "

- "Turning to . . . "

- "Another area for consideration is . . . "

Conclusion—Bring It Home, Make It Memorable!

The introduction is the first impression you make. The conclusion is almost as important because it's your last chance to leave an imprint. How well the audience remembers you and what you had to say largely depends on how you wrap things up.

Experts suggest that a good conclusion should do three things: Briefly summarize your speech, give the audience a feeling of closure (nobody likes to be left hanging), and make a good final impression. Use words that help people know you are close to the end, such as "In closing," "To wrap up," or "I have one final thought. . . ."

Make your last words memorable and help you connect solidly with the audience; make them shine. Whether you ask for help to support a good cause, make a prediction, recite a short poem or quote, or tell a story, the main thing is to do it with style.

Practice Makes Perfect

Now that you have written your speech, read it out loud at a comfortable pace. Time yourself with a watch to make sure the speech is just the right length. If it's too long, cut it now. If it's too short, do more research and put some meat on that skinny skeleton!

Some speakers like to memorize their speech so they can present it without looking at their notes. Try this when you are giving a short speech, but always take your notes with you to the stage so you don't get off track.

For longer speeches, plan to refer to your notes more often. However, the less you do this, the more attention you can pay to connecting to the audience. Small note cards work well and are less obtrusive than sheets of paper. It's safe to say the better you know your material, the more at ease you will feel.

Once you have memorized the first few minutes of your speech, stand before a mirror, look directly at yourself, and deliver the lines without using your notes. If you have a full-length mirror, this is an even better place to practice. Speak clearly without rushing. Don't be afraid to pause, and take steady breaths at natural breaks in your lines.

Look at your posture first. Are you standing straight? You don't want the audience to see you slumped over. Your carriage should be erect and proud. Have confidence in who you are and what you have to say.

What are your hands doing while you are speaking? Relax your hands, keeping them mostly at your sides and outside of your pockets. It's OK to gesture to make a point, but too much

R-E-L-A-X

Keep your shoulders relaxed. Clenching them will increase your nervousness and make you look uncomfortable and feel tense. Before you begin, relax the muscles in your back, shoulders, and hands by consciously taking several slow, deep breaths.

ınd you will appear to be flailing around. It takes a little prac- ice, but you can become comfortable with your hands relaxed ıt your sides and gesturing only when you want to draw the ıudience in to your subject at key points.

Are you having a hard time with some of the words you memorized in the opening lines? Sometimes, things that look ʒood on paper can be a lot harder to say. Rewrite anything that ‹eeps tripping you up or leaves you feeling tongue-tied.

Listen to your voice. Keep it even and speak with modula- ion. Give vocal emphasis to parts of the speech you want the ıudience to remember.

Practice the entire speech in front of the mirror every day ıntil you look and sound like someone you would like to hear. Once your speech starts coming easy enough that you don't ıave to look at your notes a lot, it's time to add a friendly ›ractice audience.

Friends and Family Make Good Practice

Before giving your speech in public, present it at home to your family or a few trusted friends. Have someone time your speech and keep track of how many times you say "um" or "ah" or anything else that is simply filler. Tell your "audience" that you will welcome comments and constructive criticism after you finish the speech and that whatever they say will only help you improve.

Chances are you don't have a podium in your living room so this will give you an opportunity to speak without a barrier between you and the audience. If you can keep your cool holding your notes and without the comfort of hiding behind a podium, speaking in front of a podium will be a snap.

Sit down in the living room and ask someone to stand up and introduce you and your topic by saying something like, "Now I'd like to introduce you to our speaker, Steve Bergen, who is going to tell us a little more about the topic of . . ."

Stand up straight and walk to the center of the room. Face your practice audience with confidence, shoulders squared, and back straight. Thank the person who introduced you, calling the person by name, and then thank your audience for coming. Holding your notes casually in your hands, deliver the speech, looking from one person to another as you speak. Focus especially on the smiling, friendly, or attentive faces in front of you—your life preservers that can keep you afloat and boost your confidence.

When you are finished, walk confidently and quietly back to your seat and sit down. Don't throw yourself in the chair like you just escaped a hail of rocks. Then ask politely how much time the speech took and how many "ums" and stammers you made.

Attention!

Shuffling is for the dance floor, slouching is for hanging out with friends. For public speaking engagements, keep your legs straight, feet slightly apart, and face your audience. If you are using visual aids, you will be moving around a little, but don't give the audience the impression you are "traveling" or flopping around. That's distracting!

Fish for Feedback

Now it's time to put on your thickest skin. Take comments and criticism from your practice audience and turn it to your advantage. Listen carefully to the feedback and don't take it personally, even if it seems hurtful or inappropriate. Thank each person who expresses an opinion, no matter how outlandish you might think it is.

Ask specific questions about the level of eye contact you achieved, how your body language looked, and how you might use your hands more effectively to make a point. Ask if you looked relaxed. Did anyone think you moved around too much, or find the number of times you looked at your notes distracting?

Review the comments and make changes to your speech based on those suggestions you think are important. If your presentation needs a number of corrections, practice some more. Then ask your family or a friend to listen to the speech again. Refining a speech and your presentation skills in this way is a lot less intimidating than doing it in front of a real audience.

Delivering Your Speech

Now that you have prepared your speech and practiced
in front of friends and family, you are ready to deliver
your speech to the intended audience.

Prepare the Room

Your first task is to prepare the room where you plan to speak.
Arrive at least an hour early. Give yourself plenty of time to
prepare mentally, and correct any mistakes in lighting, the
sound system if you are using a microphone, the seating
arrangements, and any audiovisual equipment.

If your equipment uses electrical outlets, be prepared!
Bring a three-prong/two-prong outlet adapter and an exten-
sion cord with you. You never know when you will need
one. Also bring a small flashlight or penlight in case you have
to darken the room and still need to refer to your notes.

Check the seating arrangement before anyone arrives.
If you expect 10 people and you have 40 chairs, move 30 of
them away from the area where you will be speaking. Arrange
small-group seating in a semicircle so that all participants can
see you and one another. For larger groups, seating arranged in
straight rows works best.

Sit in a chair in the front row, back row, and at the sides
of the seating arrangement. If you can, have someone stand
for a minute where you will be speaking so you can check for
distractions. Anything that looks weird or busy might draw the
audience's attention and should be removed. If you are using
visual aids, check that nothing will block the view of your
slide show or overheads, and adjust the projector accordingly.

Make sure the equipment works. Check everything twice. Be sure you know how to operate the projector and the microphone. If the projector takes a bulb, have a spare nearby in case it burns out. Use a screen as the backdrop for slide shows instead of the wall: The images will show up better.

If you are using a podium and you aren't quite tall enough to be seen over it, stand on a sturdy box or step stool. While you are on stage, before people arrive, look around for anything that distracts you. Is there a window? Close the drapes. You don't want to find yourself or the audience daydreaming or gazing outside during the presentation. How is the temperature in the room? If it's too hot or too cold, adjust it so that both you and the audience can stay focused on the presentation.

Check the lighting. If there is a dimmer switch, turn the lights on low only during the slide show or when using overheads. The images will still show up and you won't be left in the dark without your notes. If there is no dimmer switch, use your small flashlight.

Go to the restroom before you speak. Take a few deep breaths while you are there and relax your shoulders and back muscles.

The trick is not to be fussing around with anything when the audience arrives. Greet each person and shake hands. Introduce yourself if you don't know someone. The preparation process should help you feel relaxed and in control because you will know the room and will have prepared the equipment and presentation from every angle.

Making — and Leaving — a Good Impression

When the Scoutmaster or teacher introduces you, stand up and smile as you walk toward the place where you will give the speech. Shake hands with and look directly at the person who introduced you, if this is appropriate. If not, thank the person and then smile as you establish eye contact with the audience. You don't need to look like the Cheshire cat up there, but there is some truth to the phrase, "Smile and the world smiles with you." A sincere and confident smile and an upbeat introduction can melt the coldest hearts.

Stand up straight with your feet slightly apart and arms relaxed at your sides ready to emphasize a point with a gesture. Lean slightly toward your audience to show you are engaged and confident. If you still feel a little shaky, hold on to the podium, but not so tight you look like you might bench-press it through the floorboards.

Your facial expressions should reflect your position on the points you want to make. Are you telling the audience a side of the story with which you don't agree? Then frown. Are you perplexed by an argument that disagrees with your point of view? Look confused. Does something strike you as silly or overblown? Give a look of disbelief.

Did you fumble a line along the way? Slow down. Pause. Smile. Resist the urge to move on too fast. As a general rule, don't apologize. Just keep going at an even pace and regain your momentum slowly. You're human. No one expects you to be perfect, so don't expect it from yourself.

If you are giving an informative or persuasive speech, questions will likely follow. At the start of your conclusion, tell the audience that you will take questions after your concluding remarks. This will get the audience to start thinking of questions to ask. The audience will clap as soon as it's clear you are finished. After the applause, thank the audience, smile, and stride confidently off the stage and back to your seat. This is the last impression you will make. Don't let the audience know you were scared by the experience. Leave the impression that you enjoyed speaking to them.

Hand Check

Don't rock back and forth—your audience will get seasick. Standing with your hands on your hips or folding your arms across your chest are also no-win propositions—it will look as though you are about to tell them what's what. Casually putting one hand in your pocket from time to time is fine—just don't make it look like an unusable claw.

Visual Aids

Coordinate the content and timing of visual aids—slides, drawings, or product and equipment examples—with your main points. Concentrate on one slide, chart, or object at a time. The audience will need about 20 seconds to view each item to register what they have seen. Don't use too many visual aids, and keep them simple.

Slides that display words should use clean, readable type. Use uppercase letters when it is appropriate to capitalize a word; otherwise, use lowercase letters because these are easier to read than blocks of uppercase type. If you discuss a point that is not covered in your slides, turn the machine off or put a blank slide in place while you talk about that information. (The blank slide will look dark on the screen.) This way, the audience won't focus on a slide that has nothing to do with what you are saying.

On flip charts, use thick blue or black markers and make sure your writing is neat. Don't put too many words on any one slide or chart. If the audience can see it, don't read it to them word for word, but do refer to the information. Remember to check and recheck the spelling and accuracy of all information you present beforehand.

Use bar graphs to compare data and line graphs to show change over time. Flow charts can help walk the audience through a series of steps necessary to effect change.

Computers and the Internet have made slides and overheads easier to produce and use. Just be certain to number slides and overheads in advance. Drop a tray of slides or a stack of overheads before a presentation and you will quickly realize why numbering is a good practice.

May I, Please?

One important consideration before you use graphics, cartoons, or logos downloaded from the Internet, or illustrations taken from published sources: Make sure you have copyright permission to do so.

Designing Your Own Visual Aids

You don't have to be a graphic designer to create stunning visual aids. If you can use a computer, you probably have access to simple software that can make your visual aids look professional. Word processors such as Microsoft Word and Corel WordPerfect include clip art and fonts that you can use to create interesting overheads. Or try software programs designed for creating slide and overheads, such as Harvard Graphics Easy Presentations and Microsoft PowerPoint.

Desktop publishing programs intended for creating newsletters and business brochures can make overheads and slides, too. These include but aren't limited to Microsoft Publisher, Adobe PageMaker, and QuarkXpress.

How to Speak Persuasively

Do you want your words to move people to action? Change their minds? Persuade them! These powerful speaking techniques can help accomplish your goal.

Deductive Approach

State up front what you want listeners to do—vote for a candidate, save a river, host a foreign exchange student, sign up for Scouting. Then spend the rest of the speech giving reasons or arguments for doing so.

Inductive Approach

Use reasons and arguments to lead up to the conclusion, where you will tell the audience what you want them to do. This might be called the rolling thunder approach, followed by the *ka-BOOM* at the end.

One-Sided Approach

State the side of the issue for which you stand. Instead of talking about opposing views, focus on your side alone. Support your position with plenty of reasons and examples. State clearly what you want the audience to do.

Two-Sided or Multi-Faceted Approach

Most issues have more than one side. This approach addresses both sides, or perhaps, three or four different facets of an issue. Champion your side and argue against others by using fact and reason. Your chances of winning folks over to your side greatly increase when you ask them to make a small change rather than a big one.

Let Your Body Language Do the Talking

Regardless of your approach, use body language to encourage change and call people to action. In a persuasive speech, it's good to move around a little on stage and use gestures to emphasize major points. You don't want to pound the podium with your fist, but you can, for example, put your hands together in a triangle shape to draw attention to a main point. Or number the points and check them off using your fingers.

Any number of natural open gestures where your arms and hands reach out toward the audience can help draw people's attention toward you. If you can get someone to videotape your presentation during a practice run, watch the tape and take special note of your body language. How genuine do your gestures look? Does anything look wooden, forced, or just plain odd? Think about ways to improve your body language so it matches or enhances your message. The main thing to remember is that you must believe sincerely in your subject before you can persuade others to join your cause.

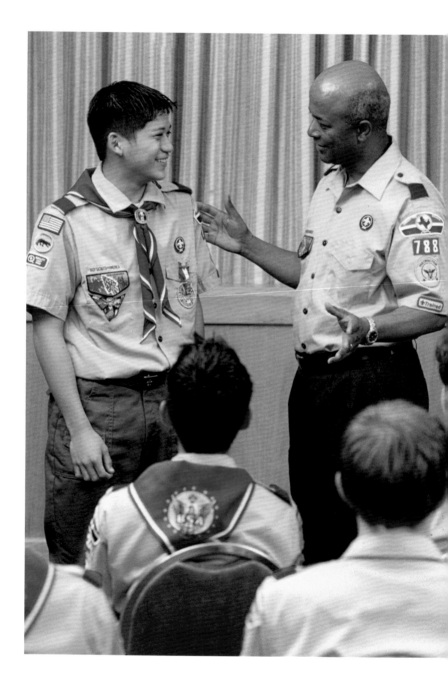

The Impromptu Speech

An impromptu speech can't really be compared with a traditional speech. It is simply a brief talk on a subject the speaker knows something about but for which he or she has had little time to prepare. Chances are, you may find yourself in this situation a couple of times a week in school.

Suppose you are at a Scout meeting and the Scoutmaster asks you, without warning, to tell the troop about plans for an upcoming campout to Three Rivers State Park. Think for a moment what you know about the campout, then quickly organize your thoughts.

Don't be afraid to pause for a second and reflect on the question or topic you have been asked to present. It will make you seem intelligent and reflective, like you are living up to the old adage, "Think before you speak." People who take a little time to ponder a response often speak wiser words than those who launch into a topic without engaging their brain first.

If you need a little time to organize your thoughts on the fly, mirror the question or topic by restating it. "You've asked me to talk to the troop about our upcoming October campout to Three Rivers State Park. . . ."

When you begin, speak clearly and concisely about the various plans for the campout. Your impromptu speech might cover what to bring, who will do the meal planning beforehand and the cooking on the trip, who is assigned to cleanup, various safety issues to consider inside the park, and lastly, where and what time to meet for departure, and what time the Scouts will return home. Remind Scouts at the end of your speech to check with their folks about volunteering as chape ones. You probably won't be asked to talk about a topic you don't know something about. Whatever the subject, keep your focus, quickly decide your purpose, make your main points, and finish up. Don't ramble on like a lonesome cowboy out on the prairie singing 79 verses of the same song to his horse.

Conclude with a brief summary or by stating the most important information the audience should remember.

Come to Order— Parliamentary Procedure Made Easy

The specific ground rules applied to formal meetings are known as *parliamentary procedure,* which allow a group, rather than an individual, to make decisions. The most common set of rules used is called Robert's Rules of Order. It is widely recognized as a fair, proper, and democratic way to run meetings. Many large and formal groups, such as the U.S. Senate and the various bodies of the United Nations, establish their own procedural rules. Some fraternal, social, civic, and business organizations accept Robert's Rules in general but provide specific exceptions in their constitutions and bylaws.

If you learn Robert's Rules, you will never be out of order because most other sets of parliamentary procedure vary little from this sturdy, time-tested set. You can find a copy of *Robert's Rules of Order Newly Revised* at your local library. The chart at the end of this chapter also can help.

Now consider the circumstances where parliamentary procedure could come in handy. In informal meetings, participants sit around a table or in a circle. When individuals have something to say, they merely speak. If participants want to ask questions of one another, they ask directly and receive a direct reply. An informal meeting operates under the rules of common courtesy.

In formal meetings, the chair, or leader, conducts all business. While the leader of an informal meeting may participate in the discussion, the chair of a formal meeting does not enter the discussion or, more properly, the debate. The chair only conducts the meeting. All speakers must first be recognized by the chair and technically, all remarks are directed to the chair. Questions from individual to individual also are directed via the chair. The formal meeting is more a debate of opposing ideas, each of which strives for audience approval. The chair enforces the rules equally on all participants to ensure that each person has a fair opportunity to present his or her point of view.

Leading Informal Discussion

While informal discussions do not have rules, the chair must apply commonsense ideas for a successful meeting to take place. No one insists that the chair apply these ideas as with more formal meetings. They just make the meeting worthwhile and productive.

Parliamentary procedure may seem arbitrary. Yet it would be impossible for a group to act without having a set procedure for deciding what the group action will be. Simply having the rules, no matter how good or poor they are, can be more important than the question of what rules to have. Fairness comes from having a standard procedure decided beforehand and applied equally to all parties.

The chair or leader of the meeting—in this case, you— should be prepared. Study the topic and prepare an opening statement briefly outlining the reason for the session. You have to get things started so always have two or three starter questions ready. Once the discussion is underway, you have completed a major portion of your task.

Your continuing responsibility is to keep the discussion going. You should not have to talk much yourself, but you can encourage presentation of new ideas and seek out friendly disagreement. Try to draw out less talkative members of the group and discourage long-winded or aimless speeches that dominate the discussion. When necessary, state that a subject is too big and would best be discussed later. Responsibility for keeping the meeting going also means keeping it focused. When the discussion begins to roam, bring the group back to the point.

Note key points people make and write down who made them. Also keep track of disagreements. Occasionally summarizing the discussion can prevent repetition or leaving plans half-completed. It also provides an opportunity to credit individual members of the group for their ideas.

As the chair, you are responsible for making a closing statement. The summary should include not only points the group agreed upon, but a statement of disagreements, too.

Chart of Parliamentary Procedure

Order of Preference (Order in which motions are taken up)	Is the Question Debatable?	Can Amen...
To fix the time to which to adjourn*	Not if there is another motion on the floor	Ye
To adjourn (without qualification)	No	N
To take a recess*	Not if there is another motion on the floor	Ye
To raise a question of rights and privileges	No	N
To lay a question on the table (to lay it aside)	No	N
Point (or question) of order	No	N
Appeal from ruling of chair	Yes, except cases involving indecorum	N
To suspend the rules	No	N
The previous question (stops debate)	No	N
To limit (or extend limit) of debate	No	Ye
To postpone consideration to a certain time	Yes	Ye
To refer to a committee	Yes	Ye
To amend an amendment	Only if the motion is	N
To amend	Only if the motion is	Ye
To postpone consideration indefinitely	Yes; also permits debate on main question	N
Any main question	Yes	Ye

*Has this order only if there is another question on the floor; if no question is on the floor, it is a mai

**A motion to reconsider can be made only by a person who voted on the winning side.

Can It Be Reconsidered?**	Required for Adoption	Is a Second Required?	Can a Speaker Be Interrupted?
Yes	Majority	Yes	No
No	Majority	Yes	No
No	Majority	Yes	No
No	Decision by chair	No	Yes
No	Majority	Yes	No
No	Decision by chair	No	Yes
Yes	Majority	Yes	Yes
No	Two-thirds	Yes	No
the main question is voted upon	Two-thirds	Yes	No
Yes	Two-thirds	Yes	No
Yes	Majority	Yes	No
fter the committee as taken it up	Majority	Yes	No
Yes	Majority	Yes	No
Yes	Majority	Yes	No
vote was affirmative	Majority	Yes	No
Yes	Majority	Yes	No

Public Speaking Resources

Scouting Literature

Journalism and *Communications* merit badge pamphlets

Books

Andrews, Robert. *The Concise Columbia Dictionary of Quotations.* Columbia University Press, 1989.

Visit the Boy Scouts of America's official retail website at http://www.scoutstuff.org for a complete listing of all merit badge pamphlets and other helpful Scouting materials and supplies.

Applewhite, Ashton, et al. *And I Quote: The Definitive Collection of Quotes, Sayings and Jokes for the Contemporary Speechmaker.* St. Martin's Press, 1992.

Detz, Joan. *It's Not What You Say, It's How You Say It.* St. Martin's Griffen, 2000.

———. *Can You Say a Few Words?* St. Martin's Press, 1991.

Griffin, Jack. *How to Say It Best: Choice Words, Phrases and Model Speeches for Every Occasion.* Prentice Hall, 1994.

Gottesman, Deb, and Buzz Mauro. *Taking Center Stage: Masterful Public Speaking Using Acting Skills You Never Knew You Had.* Berkley Books, 2001.

King, Larry. *How to Talk to Anyone, Anytime, Anywhere: The Secrets of Good Communication.* Random House Audio Publishing Inc., 1994.

Kushner, Malcolm L. *Public Speaking for Dummies.* IDG Books Worldwide Inc., 1999.

Otfinoski, Steven. *Speaking Up, Speaking Out: A Kid's Guide to Making Speeches, Oral Reports, and Conversation.* Millbrook Press, 1997.

Safire, William. *Lend Me Your Ears: Great Speeches in History.* Norton, W. W. & Company Inc., 1997.

Zimmerman, Doris P. *Robert's Rules in Plain English.* Collins, 2005.

Organizations and Websites

National Speakers Association
1500 S. Priest Drive
Tempe, AZ 85281
Telephone: 480-968-2552
Website: http://www.nsaspeaker.org

oastmasters International
3182 Arroyo Vista
ancho Santa Margarita, CA 92688
elephone: 949-858-8255
Vebsite: http://www.toastmasters.org

Vords That Shook the World
49 S. Camden Drive
everly Hills, CA 90212
elephone: 310-273-5787
Vebsite: http://www.wordsthatshook-
neworld.com

Acknowledgments

'he Boy Scouts of America greatly
ppreciates the assistance of Forrest
C. Greenslade, Ph.D., D.T.M., with
his edition of the *Public Speaking*
nerit badge pamphlet. As an active
nember of Toastmasters International,
Dr. Greenslade has earned the
Distinguished Toastmaster Award
nd was named North Carolina's
oastmaster of the year in 2001.

Many thanks to Malcolm Kushner,
uthor of *Public Speaking for Dummies,*
i funny, comprehensive guide to public
peaking. For the tips on stage fright,
he BSA acknowledges Chris Widener,
uthor, speaker, and president of Made
or Success and Extraordinary Leaders
http://www.madeforsuccess.com
nd http://www.extraordinaryleaders.
com), and Tom Antion, president of
he Advanced Public Speaking Institute
http://www.public-speaking.org),
vhich teaches advanced techniques to
nove people to action through the use
of public speaking.

We appreciate the Quicklist
Consulting Committee of the
Association for Library Service to
Children, a division of the American
Library Association, for its assistance
with updating the resources section of
this merit badge pamphlet.

We appreciate the work of
freelance writer Shannon Lowry, a
former associate editor of *Boys' Life*
magazine. She is the author of two
nonfiction books, *Northern Lights:
Tales of Alaska's Lighthouses and
Their Keepers* and *Natives of the
Far North: Alaska's Vanishing
Culture Through the Eye of
Edward Sheriff Curtis.*

Photo Credits

©Photos.com—cover *(microphone,
notebook, projector, table/chairs,
easel);* pages 27 and 32 *(all except
screen shot)*

All other photos not listed above are
the property of or are protected by the
Boy Scouts of America.

Dan Bryant—pages 18, 23 *(both)*, 25,
28–29 *(all)*, 31, 33–34 *(both)*, and 36

Darrell Byers—pages 21 and 26

Tom Copeland—cover *(Scout);*
pages 3 and 9

Doug Knutson—page 11

Randy Piland—pages 7 and 35

Notes

Notes

Notes

Notes